HECATE

MONSTERS OF MYTHOLOGY

25 VOLUMES

Hellenic

Amycus
Anteus
The Calydonian Boar
Cerberus
Chimaera
The Cyclopes
The Dragon of Beotia
The Furies
Geryon
Harpalyce
Hecate
The Hydra
Ladon
Medusa
The Minotaur
The Nemean Lion
Procrustes
Scylla and Charybdis
The Sirens
The Spear-birds
The Sphinx

Norse

Fafnir
Fenris

Celtic

Drabne of Dole
Pig's Ploughman

MONSTERS OF MYTHOLOGY

HECATE

Bernard Evslin

CHELSEA HOUSE PUBLISHERS

New York   Philadelphia

1988

EDITOR
Jennifer Caldwell

ART DIRECTOR
Giannella Garrett

PICTURE RESEARCHER
Susan Quist

DESIGNER
Victoria Tomaselli

5   7   9   8   6   4

Library of Congress Cataloging-in-Publication Data

Evslin, Bernard.
Hecate/Bernard Evslin.

p.   cm.—(Monsters of mythology)
Summary: Recounts the myth of the goddess of the
underworld known for her witchcraft and black magic.
ISBN 1-55546-252-9
1. Hecate (Greek deity)—Juvenile literature.   [1. Hecate (Greek
deity) 2. Mythology, Greek.] I. Title.   II. Series: Evslin,
Bernard. Monsters of mythology.
BL820.H43E87   1987
398.2′1—dc19   87-16010

Printed in Mexico.

For my daughter,
JANET
whose magic hands and healing beauty
make the harpies fly.

Characters

Monsters

Hecate (HECK uh tee)	Queen of the Harpies
Harpies (HAHR pihz)	Demonic crones who police the underworld
Cyclopes (SY kloh peez)	Powerful one-eyed servants of the gods
Hundred-handed Giants	Also employed by the gods
Serpent	A huge snake who works for Hades in Tartarus

Gods

Zeus (ZOOS)	King of the Gods
Hades (HAY deez)	His brother; ruler of the Land Beyond Death

Dionysus (dy un NY sus)	Son of Zeus; the vine god
Artemis (AHR tuh mihs)	Daughter of Zeus; the moon goddess

Mortals

Orpheus (OR fee uhs)	Poet and musician whom death did not silence
Eurydice (yoo RIHD ih see)	His bride
Asclepius (ass KLEE pee uhs)	Son of Apollo, the sun god; father of medicine
Telesphora (tuh LEHS fuh ruh)	Assistant to Asclepius; a magical nurse
Vine-tenders	Countrymen who practice the rites of human sacrifice
Thallo (THUH loh)	A crippled poet

The Tormented

Shades	Souls of the dead
Tantalus (TAN tuh luhs)	A sinner; always desiring, always denied
Tityus (TIHT ih uhs)	A Titan who led a revolt against Zeus

Sisyphus (SIHS ih fuhs)	Another who offended the gods and by result is bound to an endless task
Stone man	A hero who was turned to stone after death
Stone woman	His wife, a huntress, also petrified in stone

Animals

Shade of a war-horse	Who served loyally in life and in death
Stone dog	Who followed his master and mistress into Tartarus

Contents

CHAPTER I

Death's Domain   1

CHAPTER II

The Poet   9

CHAPTER III

The Cannibal Gods   15

CHAPTER IV

His Song Is a Mischief   21

CHAPTER V

The Hag Hovers   27

CHAPTER VI

Eurydice   33

CHAPTER VII

The Healer   39

CHAPTER VIII

The Strangler   43

CHAPTER IX

The Singing Head   53

CHAPTER X

The Rebel Shade   61

CHAPTER XI

The Descent   67

CHAPTER XII

A Hellish Battle   75

1

Death's Domain

ecate was Queen of the Harpies. And what were the Harpies? They were the flying hags who patrolled the holding pens and roasting pits of the Land Beyond Death.

Hecate's mother was a nymph of the Falcon clan, her father an Egyptian panther-god. Those of her victims who survived stammered out different stories. But most sources agree that she looked like a cheetah partially transformed into a woman—long-legged, long armed, with blazing yellow eyes, teeth like ivory knives, and hands and feet tipped with great ripping claws.

Hecate was called the High Hag, a title rather than a description. Though white haired, she was always in the prime of her strength. These white locks straggling about her stern young face only added to the terror of her appearance.

Her wings were ribbed and made of membranous leather, tinged gold, wherein arose the report that she wore brass wings. Her followers, the Harpies, did have brass wings and brass claws and were true hags, with hideous ravaged faces. But she, their queen, was beautiful as a cheetah in mid leap, if that which murders can be described as beautiful.

To understand Hecate's duties, and the workings of that region of hell called Tartarus, we must go back to the beginning of Zeus's reign, when he was still deciding what kind of world he wanted.

He was seated upon his new throne, a royal perch carved out of the rock that formed the peak of Mount Olympus. On a clear day, it appeared to those below that the whole mighty mountain was a throne for the King of the Gods, and the great plain his footstool.

The towering black-robed figure of Zeus's brother, Hades, stood beside the throne. The two gods were conversing earnestly.

"These humans must learn that our displeasure will become their pain," Zeus declared.

"A start," said Hades. "But not enough."

"What do you mean?"

"Being mortal," said Hades, "they view everything as temporary. They know that when they cease, their troubles cease also. And this encourages them to ignore consequence."

"Not if the consequence is sufficiently painful," said Zeus.

"I beg to differ, O king and brother. The bravest and strongest are able to endure whatever torment we visit upon them because they know that death will end their suffering."

"Surely," said Zeus, "you are not proposing that we grant them immortality?"

"Indeed not. Immortality must be reserved for us gods. But we can extend the human capacity for suffering so that it may persist beyond physical death. Thus, we shall be able to arrange a system of endless punishment that will frighten mankind into docility."

"But," said Zeus, "won't the prospect of eternal suffering make them hate us?"

"Quite the contrary," said Hades. "When people are sufficiently terrified, they tend to adore those who can hurt them but sometimes refrain."

"Hades, I like your thinking!"

"Futhermore, brother," said Hades, "since the logic of my idea seems to indicate the need for a vast prison compound where the dead can serve out their sentences, I hereby volunteer to rule that realm."

"Do you? It seems a dismal chore for my eldest brother."

"I see it differently. Such a realm, a dance with demons, made brilliant by pain, is exactly what I am meant to rule."

So Hades was appointed King of the Dead, and given the vast gloomy hollow of the underearth as his domain. He immediately named Hecate his chief aide. He borrowed the tribe of one-eyed Cyclopes and a band of Hundred-handed Giants from his brother's kingdom, and kept them working night and day to remodel the place according to his design.

Before real work could begin, however, the savage creatures that dwelt underground had to be killed, captured, or

Hades was appointed King of the Dead, and given the vast gloomy hollow of the underearth as his domain.

tamed. And so the workers became warriors first—a role they welcomed.

Dragons dwelt underground. They were huge, had wings and claws and terrible teeth, wore armored hide and spiked tails, and spat fire. The Giants and Cyclopes could make no headway against the dragons. But then Hecate found a way to subdue them.

Studying the habits of the gigantic lizards, she found that their dispositions were so foul that they were forced to nest one to a cave, otherwise they would fight to the death. Thereupon she led a raiding party against one nest at a time until she had captured six dragons.

She then assigned four of the Hundred-handed Giants to each dragon. Gripped by four hundred hands, the creature was held high and used as a flamethrower. Thus, Hecate was able to lead her Giants and six captive dragons against the dragon swarm.

Now these creatures, for all their size, had brains no larger than walnuts. Seeing their own kind spit fire at them, they began to fight among themselves, killing each other off until only a few were left.

The surviving dragons were driven from their caves into the upper world, where they began to prey on humans—which pleased Hades, for their kills enlarged his kingdom.

Still using the captive dragons as flamethrowers, the Giants and the Cyclopes tamed the enormous serpents that also dwelt underground. Hecate then trained them to guard the outlying regions of Tartarus.

Hades bade the Cyclopes build him a palace under a great seam of coal that looked like the night sky. He commissioned his nephew, Hephaestus, the smith god, to make a silver moon that worked by invisible springs and pulleys, and climbed and sank and changed shape and color like the real moon. And the Cyclopes stuck diamonds into the black dome to imitate stars.

A grove was planted about the palace, and was named Erebus. Beautiful mournful trees grew there—alder and myrtle and weeping willow. Ghostly deer glimmered among the trees. Black swans swam on a black lake; only their glittering eyes could be seen, and their white masks.

All this time, Hecate and her band of hell-hags, the Harpies, were overseeing another party of Cyclopes and Giants, who were constructing the roasting pits and torture pens of Tartarus, and stoking the furnaces for a Lake of Fire that burned with a perpetual flame. The banks of this lake were diabolically contrived to recede before a swimmer trying to reach shore.

When all was completed, Hades demanded a secret entrance to his realm so that none might enter but the dead. He chose a lake in the Saronic mountains, and had the Cyclopes and Giants empty it of its cold blue waters. Then they drove a great cleft into the dry bed. Hades named the chasm Avernus after the vanished lake. It led down through a series of interlocked caves—down, down, to the bank of the River Styx, which had been bent out of its course and made to flow underground.

Hades named the chasm Avernus after the vanished lake. It led down through a series of interlocked caves . . . to the banks of the River Styxx.

In fact, the mighty laborers had twisted the routes of four rivers and forced them into subterranean channels, forming the boundaries of the Land Beyond Death. The rivers were named Styx, Acheron, Phlegethon, and Cocytus—or Hatred, War, Fire, and Wailing Waters.

The Harpies acted as ushers . . . showing off the new devices like the Barbed Flick, the Marrow Log and the Gut-winder.

Now, Hades was eager to display his new domain. He invited the entire assembly of the gods underground. Also invited were the minor gods—the Muses, the Graces, the Hours; Hypnos, God of Sleep; the wood god, Pan, and his band of Satyrs; the wind god, Aeolus, and his Four Winds; the beautiful flame-haired Eos, Goddess of the Dawn; the crusty old sea deities who aided Poseidon—Proteus, Nereus, and Triton with his twisted horn. And those three crone sisters, the Fates, hobbled down; they added nothing to any celebration but no one dared offend them.

The Harpies acted as ushers, leading their distinguished visitors through the roasting pits and torture pens, showing off new devices like the Barbed Flick, the Marrow Log, and the Gut-winder. Hecate took charge of the most honored guests, Zeus, Hera, and Poseidon, explaining each improvement, showing them about the entire perimeter of the Lake of Fire, and introducing them to the charred turnspit demons and the faceless Torment Team.

After the grand tour, the guests were led to the palace grounds at Erebus, where they were treated to the spectacle of a Harpy echelon flying up into the black vault and plucking diamond stars out of the dome. Then, the Harpies, led by Hecate, swooped down and presented a diamond to each guest. Hecate presented Zeus with an enormous gem, and Hera with its twin.

6

Zeus laughed with pleasure and embraced Hades as all the company cheered. Then he drew him aside for a private talk.

"You've done a marvelous job down here," said Zeus. "There's only one thing I might suggest."

"Name it, Majesty, and it shall be done."

"Well, it's a difficult matter and requires thought. As things stand now, no living mortal can enter your realm, nor dead ones depart. So there is no way for the human herd to understand what happens after death to those who displease us."

"O king and brother," said Hades, "I have reason to believe that the torments we are preparing will be so intense that a sense of anguish will steam up from this place and seep through the earth's crust into the consciousness of humankind—perhaps in the form of dreams, premonitions, the ravings of oracles."

"All very well," said Zeus, "but I believe we shall need more positive testimony. No hurry though; we'll both give it some thought. And now, brother, let me congratulate you again. This hell you are making promises to be the most splendid piece of work since we built the heavens."

2

The Poet

Once it became known that the end of life did not mean the end of suffering, and that divine vengeance would continue to pursue offenders even after death, people were gripped by such terror that they sought to placate the gods by every means imaginable, including human sacrifice.

Thus, in response to any natural disaster—earthquake, tidal wave, volcano, drought or famine—people, made cruel by fear, would select a victim. It could be man, woman, or child— sometimes an entire family. They would be dragged to the altar and put to the sword before an image of whatever god or goddess was to be appeased. Nor were those who did the killing always moved by religious impulse. This custom of human sacrifice was also a useful way to work off a grudge or settle a quarrel.

And since natural disasters always blew over after a time, those who preached sacrifice could boast of a string of successes. So the habit grew. Certain blood offerings embedded themselves in custom, became ritual, practiced not only in times of trouble, but in times of prosperity to buy a god's favor in advance. Before a fishing fleet embarked, for example, some villager might be chosen as an offering to Poseidon. The victim would be taken to the altar of the sea god and stabbed to death with a knife carved of whale's ivory. The shrieks of the victim and his family would be drowned by the prayers of those calling to Poseidon for a rich harvest of fish.

Before every Spring Sowing, the strongest and most beautiful youths of a village would be brought to the ploughed field and butchered with a scythe—so that strong blood might nourish the furrows and bribe Demeter, Goddess of Growing Things, to send fat crops.

Most of the gods, while pretending disapproval, secretly relished these blood offerings. Hades, of course, openly approved, for corpses enlarged his kingdom.

10

Most of the gods, while pretending disapproval, secretly relished these blood offerings.

As Orpheus strolled about, plucking at his lyre . . .
savage beasts and gentle beasts would come out
of the forest and stand in a circle about him.

But there was one young man who loathed the murderous rite, and risked his life again and again by trying to stop it. He was the poet, Orpheus, the first of his kind, and there has been none greater since.

A slender, graceful youth with burning black eyes, Orpheus ambled about as if sleepwalking, but could move very quickly on occasion. He invented the seven-string lyre and drew such ravishing melodies from it that trees would wrench themselves out of the earth and hobble about on their roots to follow him. And as he strolled about, plucking at his lyre and fitting his own verses to the music, savage beasts and gentle beasts would come out of the forest and stand in a circle about him. The wolves did

Orpheus vowed never to sail on
any ship belonging to a village
that sacrificed its sons and daughters.

not hunt, nor the deer flee. But all stood in an enchanted truce, listening.

Born in Thrace, Orpheus roamed the land, never staying long in one place. He reached the coast, and wandered the length of it, but then, instead of striking inland, turned, and began to drift down again, still following the shoreline but now stopping at each village.

The fishermen welcomed him very warmly and fought for the privilege of taking him on board their boats. Not that they were such ardent music lovers, but they knew that when he stood on their decks, plucking his lyre and singing, fish would rise from the depths and balance themselves on their tails, listening. And such fish were easy to catch. But often, as it happened, the fishermen themselves fell into a trance and forgot to cast their nets.

It was at this time that Orpheus began to attack the practice of human sacrifice. During a visit to one village, he had seen a shouting mob escort a fisherlad to the edge of a cliff. The tall, fresh-faced boy held himself erect, gazing out to sea, as the villagers chanted prayers to Earth-Shaking Poseidon, Sender of Fish. Holding his head high, the boy stood there, outfacing death, wincing only when he heard his mother sob.

Then, without waiting to be pushed, he shouted, "Accept me, O sea!" and leaped off the cliff into the swirling water below. Jumping into water from that height is like falling onto rock, and the broken body spun a few times in the riptide, then sank. The boy's mother tried to leap off after him, but was caught by her husband and led gently downhill.

Orpheus, watching, was riven to the heart. More than anything else, he was moved by the gallantry of the doomed youth who had tried so hard to welcome death, knowing that the gods preferred an offering untainted by grief or fear. Then and there, Orpheus vowed never to sail on any ship belonging to a village that sacrificed its sons and daughters.

The practical fisherfolk, faced with a choice between the immediate results of the poet's deck music and some future prospect of Poseidon's favor, chose Orpheus. So the ivory knives tasted no more innocent blood, nor were any more youths forced to leap off cliffs—at least not while the poet lingered on the coast.

3

The Cannibal Gods

rpheus traveled up and down the shore, hurling verse against the cannibal gods, and where he passed, lives were saved. After some months, however, he decided to leave the fishing villages and strike inland.

Any journey was perilous in those days. To go among strangers was to invite robbery and death. And of all places in the world, none were more murderously inhospitable than the slopes and passes of the Thracian mountains. There were bandits who routinely preyed on travelers; savage mountain clansmen who viewed everyone born outside their village as an enemy. And most dangerous of all were neither bandits nor clansmen, but the dour hardworking vine tenders whose grapes yielded a sweet potent wine.

These growers believed that the Mistress of the Crops became a ravening white sow in the summer, whose hunger could be glutted only by human flesh and whose thirst could be quenched only by blood. The Midsummer Sow had to be pleased or she would blight the grapes. Given her fill of meat and drink, however, she would load the vine with heavy purple fruit, and its juice thereof would be sweet and strong.

At midsummer, then, the vine tenders put on green clothing so they might not be seen among the leaves, and lay in wait for strangers passing by. They preferred to sacrifice at noon. They bound their victim with vines, and offered his best parts to the goddess. The head would be buried near a tumbling stream, the hands under a myrtle, and the rest of the body put into a shallow hole among the vine roots.

Orpheus, new to these slopes and a stranger to local custom, was pacing gaily down the trail, admiring the steep, terraced fields that seemed to be tilted toward the rich sunlight. He was hot and thirsty. Perching on a low stone wall, he plucked some grapes. They were sour but eased his thirst. He was cramming a handful into his mouth when the green-clad men leaped out of the brush.

They seized him. They were big, and there were three of them. He was helpless in their grip. One man held him from behind as a second stripped off his tunic. The third man stood by, holding a curved knife. They bound him to a tree, wrapping him with vines.

His lyre had dropped to the ground. The men did not know what the strange object was; they thought it some kind of weapon. One man kicked it away and was startled when the thing uttered a musical complaint. They were more startled when the trussed man uttered the same sound. They were used to their captive screaming when he saw the knife, but this one did not scream; he sang.

Birds were calling all the while. The bound man's voice threaded among them. The man with the knife tried to come closer, close enough to cut. But he could not move. His feet were rooted to the ground. The song was casting silver loops about him. He just stood there, listening. The two other men stood rooted also, listening.

Orpheus sang. His song told them that they were offering to the wrong god, that they should be worshipping no ugly, greedy midsummer sow, but *Dionysius*, Lord of the Vine, Master of Revels, Bestower of Ecstasy.

Most dangerous of all were neither bandits nor clansmen, but the dour hardworking vine tenders whose grapes yielded a sweet potent wine.

He sang of the birth of Dionysius—how his mother, a Phrygian princess named Semele, Priestess of the New Moon, was courted by Zeus, disguised as the night wind. But Semele was very proud of being loved by a god and wanted everyone to know. She coaxed Zeus into dropping his disguise. He appeared to her in his own form; she was consumed by the divine fire upon which no mortal can look, and live. . . . Dying, she gave birth to Dionysius, who was born among the flames. Ever afterward, fire ran in his veins, giving him his matchless radiance.

In his youth, Dionysius was tutored by satyrs and learned the secret of the grape and the terrible enchantment cast by its fermented juice.

"Yes!" sang Orpheus, "It is this radiant youth who empowers the vine. It is he who bestows the grape, and sweetens its juice, and lays magic upon it as it ages in the cask. It is he, Dionysius, not the Midsummer Sow."

The green-clad men knew they were listening to sacrilege and would pay with their lives when the white sow came, claiming vengeance. They knew they should move upon the singer and dismember him—offer him, piece by piece, to the raging sow, begging her forgiveness all the while. They tried to break the spell, tried to rush at Orpheus. But the song noosed them in its silver coils and they could not move.

Now, animals had slid out of the forest and stood with them, listening. Wolves and deer, and a single bear. The birds had fallen still, for they too wanted to hear, and the voice of the singer was the only sound in the hot silence of the afternoon.

Orpheus kept chanting. His song told how the youngest god Dionysius wandered far, visiting all the kingdoms that border

the Inner Sea, introducing men to the culture of the vine. He was followed by a troupe of laughing worshipers, men and women, who reveled nightly under the moon.

And now the rooted men shuddered and the animals bristled as they heard his voice take on a new tone. Trumpets rang in it—spear shock, and battle cry.

"Beware! Beware!" sang Orpheus, "One day, the vine god was captured by pirates who took him aboard their ship, thinking he was a prince they

"It is Dionysus, the radiant youth,
who empowers the vine . . .
bestows the grape, and
sweetens its juice . . ."

could hold for ransom. Then the ship stopped, though it was in deep water and sailing before the wind. Vines sprouted out of the sea, climbing the hull, twining around the mast. The oars of the galley slaves turned into sea serpents; they wrenched themselves free and swam away. Where Dionysius had been standing at the bow, a lion appeared. The wind in the rigging became the sound of flutes. The golden lion stood on his hind legs and danced. The terrified pirates jumped overboard and drowned. Beware! Beware!"

At this point in the song, a wild boar wandered out of the copse and stood among the other animals, listening. And the green-clad men, seeing the beast, thought that the sow had sent her consort to kill them. Now terror broke the spell of the music. The animals, smelling fear, began to growl. The man with the knife dropped his blade and ran. The others scurried after him, whimpering with fear. The wolves would have followed the men and torn them to pieces, but Orpheus began to sing again, for he did not wish them to be killed. He wanted no death in the grove that afternoon.

The wolves turned again, and listened to the song. And, Orpheus, escorted by wolves and the single bear, wandered the mountain villages, singing against the white sow and human sacrifice, hymning the vine god and the life-giving power of the Sun, who is the daily risen god, and can alone decree abundance.

By now, rumor of Orpheus and his band of enchanted listeners had reached the gods—those who dwelt upon Olympus, and those who prowled the depths of Tartarus. And demonish powers he hardly even knew existed began to make decisions about him.

4

His Song Is a Mischief

he roots of mountains are the roof beams of hell. Thick shafts of rock grip the floor of Hades' realm and soar upward out of sight— up through bottomless lakes and nameless caverns, lifting themselves up past the clouds into a great drench of sunlight, becoming the mountains of earth whose snowdrifts are the source of rivers, whose crags are a nest for eagles, and upon whose slopes wild horses graze.

But seen from the floor of Tartarus, they are huge pillars of rock thrusting straight up and losing themselves in darkness. Hades leaned now against one of these pillars, awaiting Hecate, whom he had summoned. He heard the chiming of brass wings before he saw the hags. He looked up. Wings and claws gleamed in the perpetual dusk. Hecate glided down, motioning for the Harpies to fly on. She coasted to the ground and alighted near Hades.

"You summoned me, my lord, and I am here."

"We have heavy matters to consider," said Hades. "Does the name Orpheus mean anything to you?"

"Is he down here?"

"No. He still lives."

"I have been so busy carrying out your instructions, O Master, that I have quite lost track of what is happening on earth."

"Well, good Hecate, I may have to enlarge your field of operations. You are the only one of my staff who has the wit to do my business on alien soil."

"I am highly gratified by your confidence in me, my lord."

"This Orpheus is a young poet," said Hades. "A Thracian."

"A poet? How does a poet come to occupy your majestic attention? I have always considered them the lightest of lightweights."

"Not this one," said Hades. "He doesn't twitter mindlessly like a bird. His song is a mischief. He wanders the land, persuading people to stop killing each other on our altars. Human sacrifice, he tells them, is a fancy name for murder. And murder, despite all natural instincts, is wrong, wrong, wrong."

"The man's a lunatic!" cried Hecate. "Why do people believe him?"

"It's because he doesn't preach," said Hades. "He's never boring. He doesn't moralize about killing, but praises life in terms so compelling that people quell their own murderous instincts. His message is gilded by such beautiful sound that it pierces the hearts of his listeners, and they refuse to do what he disapproves of. And so, he has reduced our quota of corpses."

"Truly," muttered Hecate. "The antics of this madman demand drastic action. Shall I go up there and kill him and drag his shade down here for appropriate torment?"

"No," said Hades. "I want him, but I want him alive."

"I don't understand."

"There's something I haven't discussed with you," said Hades. "It is the opinion of Zeus, which I am beginning to share, that for once we must violate our own rule. A living mortal will be permitted to visit us, and depart, alive."

"Whatever for?"

"We need a witness—one who will observe what happens down here, and return to the upper world. His testimony, it is

Wings and claws gleamed in the perpetual dusk. Hecate glided down . . .

hoped, will frighten those restless herds into the kind of docility we have never been able to impose.''

    ''I see,'' said Hecate. ''And you think that this Orpheus will make a good witness?''

    ''He is a poet. His perceptions are keen, and his testimony eloquent.''

"I want him," said Hades, "but I want him alive."

"But he's a troublemaker, you say. A very active one. Shall we not be presenting him with more opportunity for mischief?"

"I am hoping that what he sees here will frighten the mischief out of him. Besides, you, my dear Hecate, will be watching everything he does, and will be ready to pounce, should he get out of line."

"How shall we get him down here?"

"The same way we tempted the three-headed dog to these regions. We shall contrive the death of someone Orpheus loves. His passionate nature should lead him to follow her shade down to Tartarus."

"You say 'she,' " said Hecate. "Does he have a wife?"

"He does not."

"Does he love anyone?"

"I am told he does not."

"Then whom can be used as a hostage?"

"I leave the details to you, O Hag. You must arrange for him to fall in love. Poets are supposed to be inflammable, after all. And you have proved yourself a creature of infinite resource."

"Not so infinite as you suppose, my king. But I have never yet shirked a difficult assignment."

"Consequently," said Hades, "I shall expect to see this damned versifier down here as soon as our torments are in full swing."

5

The Hag Hovers

Hecate went to work immediately. She contrived matters so that nymphs thronged the path of the poet wherever he went. Orpheus was delighted by the beautiful sleek creatures, who seemed to crystallize themselves out of his song. He sported in the sea with nereids, frolicked with meadow nymphs, danced in the grove with dryads, and went bounding from rock to rock with the lithe mountain nymphs called oreads.

He welcomed them all, reveled in their company, wrapped himself in their mixed fragrances, flowered under their touch—but fixed his affections on no one. He never stayed anywhere for more than a day and a night, but kept following his restless spirit to places he had not yet seen.

But he never forgot any of the nymphs he had met, for he forgot nothing, and wove each adventure into song.

Hecate hovered invisibly, watching Orpheus, waiting for him to fall deeply in love with someone—she watched as he flitted from blossom to blossom like a bee gathering honey. For all her ferocity, she kept her patience as only a good hunter can. Nevertheless, Hecate realized that if she did not produce results she might fall into disfavor with her moody king as quickly as she had climbed into his good graces.

*Orpheus never forgot any of the nymphs he had met, for
he forgot nothing, and wove each adventure into song.*

"This one's not like other mortals," Hecate thought to herself. "He has a low boiling point, but is slow to commit himself. What I need is expert advice. I'll go to Mount Helicon where poets swarm. I'll find one there who's clever enough to tell me what I need to know, and squeeze some information out of him."

Hecate hovered invisibly over the slope of Helicon, watching a straggle of men and youths wandering about picking flowers, mumbling verse, and trying to work up nerve enough to mount the winged horse, Pegasus, who always bucked them off.

Hecate noticed one small man with twisted legs who sat on a rock watching the others, smiling to himself. "That's the one

I want," she thought. Swooping down, she caught him in her claws and carried him up the mountain to a place where no one walked. Becoming visible, she held him in one hand as she pulled the whip from her belt with the other. She drove the stock deep into the ground, then tied its long lash about his ankle, so that he was tethered like a goat.

She was amazed to see that he was still smiling, and more joyfully than ever.

"What's your name?"

"Thallo. And you are Hecate."

"How do you know?"

"I have dreamed of you. But you are more overwhelming in the flesh. I am delighted to be your captive and beseech you not to release me."

"Indeed? People do not usually welcome my attentions."

"More fools they!" cried Thallo.

"Well, little man, you're as clever as you look, aren't you? And I need your counsel."

"Glad to serve you, Goddess."

"I have a friend who is very eager to marry off her son, who is a poet."

"Does the son share his mother's enthusiasm for wedlock?" asked Thallo.

"That's just it. He's fond of girls, but in a general sort of way. He hasn't fixed his fancy on any of them."

"Well, he's young, you say."

"Not that young. Plenty old enough to settle down."

"No, my lady. Poets retain a certain childishness in such matters. That's how we manage to see the world fresh each time. We tend to look upon marriage as a trap, and babies as a burden."

"Really? I thought you fellows were of passion all compounded. Generous, tender, reckless in the heat of love, ready to dare anything?"

"That's the other side of it," said Thallo. "And if your friend's son should happen to meet a girl who inspires such passion, then, no doubt, he will make his mother happy by entering wedlock, and his wife's parents equally miserable."

"Well," said Hecate, "I don't see why the young fellow hasn't found anyone to kindle his heart. He has met all the most beautiful nymphs of his generation—nereids, naiads, dryads, oreads—one more ravishing than the next."

"And did any of these gorgeous, sportive creatures hold still long enough to listen to his verse?"

Hecate hovered invisibly over the slope of
Helicon, watching a straggle of men and
youths wandering about picking flowers, mumbling verse . . .

"What do you mean?"

"Any girl who hopes to snare a poet, my Queen, must adore poetry, *his* poetry in particular, or be able to imitate ecstasy while he intones his verse—at least until she has him married tight and fast."

"Tell me more."

"Well, it'll help if she's good-looking—with big eyes, and a trick of widening them while she listens, as if she were actually watching the words dance on air."

"Must she be a brilliant conversationalist?" asked Hecate.

"She'll need only four short phrases: 'Sing it again' . . . 'Don't stop' . . . 'Oh, marvelous!' . . . and the all-purpose 'Yes, dear.' "

"You mean she can be an imbecile just as long as she's pretty and submissive?"

"Nobody good-looking is quite an imbecile. Beauty is the body's intelligence. And when a brainy cripple tells you this, it has to be true."

"I'm not convinced," said Hecate.

"Besides, the poet is a weaver of fantasy. Whatever she lacks he will tell himself he doesn't want. We all invent our lovers, especially when young."

Hecate smiled at the little man. "You're brilliant, Thallo! If you were a few feet taller, I'd marry you myself."

"Don't decide against me too hastily, dear Hecate. I might grow on you."

6

Eurydice

Orpheus came down from the mountains into the lowlands. He wandered from village to village, playing his lyre and singing his songs. Animals followed him as he went; trees pulled themselves out of the earth and hobbled after him. Fishermen came ashore, farmers left their plows. Hordes of people were following him now as he strolled about, playing and singing. Grown men and women, boys and girls. But as time passed and the faces changed, he noted that one face was always the same. It belonged to a young girl with eyes so big, so full of light that they seemed to linger after she left, burning holes in the dusk.

And when Orpheus went into the woods again, and his audience became animals and trees, there she was too, listening. She was very slender, with a shining fall of black hair and huge black eyes. And noon and dusk and under the moon her face seemed to gather all the light there was.

Orpheus took the girl aside and spoke to her. Her name was Eurydice, she told him. But it didn't matter where she had lived, because she would never go back there. Her home would be where he was. She would follow him everywhere, and if he could not love her, she would make no demands, but follow him

anyway and listen to him sing, and serve him in any way he wished.

This is the kind of thing any man in any age likes to hear but seldom does, and never for long. A young poet hearing such praise can go absolutely drunk with joy; old ones too. Now, Orpheus had met many nymphs and beautiful young women, but he decided that this was the one he must have, this childish one with her great doelike eyes and murmuring voice and superb taste in verse. And so he married her.

All this time, Hecate hovered but did not strike. It was she who had found Eurydice and realized her possibilities, tutored her through dreams, and then finally guided her into Orpheus's path. Hecate watched them fall in love and set up housekeeping in a thatched hut on the riverbank. The Harpy hovered but did not strike. She wanted Orpheus to live a while with his new bride. She wanted love to sink its hooks deep into his heart.

Then, at last, Hecate decided the time had come. One morning when Eurydice was out picking berries, the Harpy led a savage-tempered bear toward the blackberry bush. The famished beast arose to his enormous height and loomed over the girl. Eurydice stared up in fright.

Then the bear realized that this girl belonged to Orpheus, whose singing pleased him so. His growl changed to a snuffle. He dropped to all fours and shambled away.

Hecate was not pleased. "All the beasts in this place have been corrupted by that silly music," she said to herself. "I'll have to find something less appreciative. A snake perhaps? Some of them are musical, but they dwell in holes and may not have heard the Orphic songs. I know . . . a viper! A green viper. Its brain is the size of a pea, and it's tone-deaf besides. And its venom is absolutely deadly.''

Hecate flew to a certain cave and dug out a tangle of green vipers. She plucked one loose and carried it by its tail, flying to

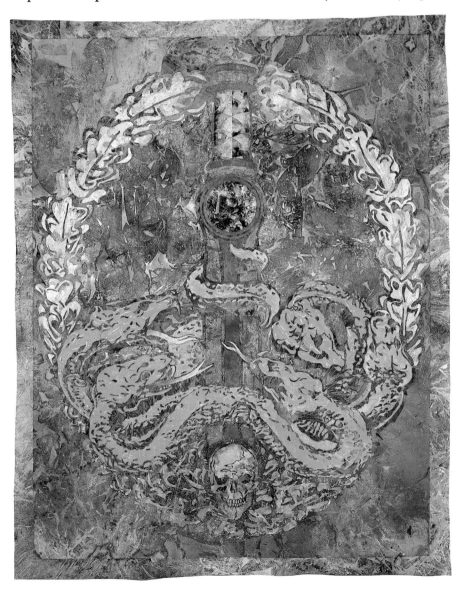

Hecate flew to a certain cave and dug out a tangle of . . . vipers.

An enormous error had been made, an unbearable discord at the very core of things.

the blackberry bush where Eurydice was still picking. The girl had eaten a berry for every one she put in the basket, and her lips were stained blue.

Hecate dropped the snake at the girl's feet. The viper, furious at being handled in such a way, reared its head and struck at the nearest living thing— which was Eurydice. It sank its teeth into her taut, scratched leg, and shot its poison. The girl stiffened and fell.

Orpheus came home and found the house empty. He waited, but Eurydice did not return. He went looking for her. He ran through the woods, searching, calling. But he could not find her. Then, Hecate perched in a tree over the fallen Eurydice and raised her voice, imitating the girl. Orpheus rushed toward the sound.

He saw something on the ground. He knelt. He refused to believe what he saw. This could not be. She couldn't be lying there like that, arms and legs still, eyes quenched. That slender face, blue smeared, was the face of a child eating berries. Death did not suit her, not at all. It could not be and must not be. It was unacceptable. An enormous error had been made, an unbearable discord at the very core of things.

He would have to go tune the world again, or it would have no place for him. He would go down to Tartarus to reclaim his wife's shade and stuff it back into her unblemished body. Then he would take her to the little house near the river.

Murmuring, "I'll be back soon," Orpheus kissed her cold brow and rushed off. He didn't know where Avernus was, but knew he would find it. In the Land Beyond Death, he would seek the ghost of his murdered bride.

7

The Healer

ut there was one who caused Hades more trouble even than Orpheus; he was Asclepius, the greatest doctor who ever lived. His father was Apollo, the sun god, also God of Music and Medicine. His mother had been a Lapith princess, named Coronis, who hated Apollo because he had abducted her on her wedding night. She ran away from Apollo and rejoined her young husband—saddening the sun god, and, what was worse, enraging his twin sister, Artemis, Goddess of the Moon. Artemis, although only 15 minutes older than her brother, had always considered herself his protector. She sped to Arcadia where the young couple had fled and slew them with her silver arrows.

Asclepius was born during his mother's death throes. But, destined for the healing arts, he had begun his study of anatomy while still in the womb. And continued to watch the events of his own birth with such intense concentration that he uttered no cry—making his midwife think that he had been born dead.

Hermes, who had always been the kindliest god, heard about the incredibly gifted child, who was his own nephew. He took charge of the babe and gave him to the Centaurs to raise.

These hill dwellers, the fabled pony-spooks
of Thessaly . . . taught the boy all they knew.

These hill dwellers, the fabled pony-spooks of Thessaly, knew more about herbs, poisonous and benign, than any other living creatures. And they taught the boy all they knew.

Asclepius developed other skills as well. He dosed and splinted, presided over the birth of the Centaur colts, and began to practice battlefield surgery at a very early age. There was plenty of need for this; his adopted tribe was quarrelsome and incredibly rash, always charging out of the hills to fight with the Lapiths of the plain—although vastly outnumbered.

After learning all he could, Asclepius left the Centaurs and began to wander the land, patching broken bodies wherever he found them.

As his talent ripened, he found himself calling on all the powers he had inherited from his father. Sunlight and music, he found, were the best medicines. He forbade his patients to lie in the dark, thinking sad thoughts, but dragged their pallets outside so that the brilliant sunlight could soak into them. Founding his own hospital, a collection of wicker huts set in a large garden on the bank of a river, he filled it with music. At all hours, the patients could hear the natural music of wind-song and birdcall; at certain hours, the flute and lyre, and voices singing. For Asclepius hired musicians, and recruited men and women with beautiful voices, and taught them to chant the praise-songs of Orpheus at sunrise and sunset and blazing noon.

Legends, of course, sprang up about the young doctor. It was said that he had been given a set of scalpels by his uncle Hephaestus, the smith god. It was said that he had stolen a skein of the vital thread used by his ancient cousins, the Fates, and that with such magically sharp knives and magically strong thread could cut someone open, whisk out a diseased organ, and sew the incision up faster than a fisherman could shuck an oyster.

Asclepius laughed when he heard these tales, but did not encourage them. He disliked cutting, and did so only when all else failed.

8

The Strangler

By this time, the song Orpheus was singing in the Land Beyond Death had begun to enter the four infernal rivers and on through underground streams to the rivers of earth. Reeds that grew upon the river banks soaked this song up through their roots. And when the wind moved among them, the reeds uttered the song anew. People, hearing it, learned for the first time what was happening to those who had died. Whoever learned about the torments of hell told others; and the dreadful news spread. The dead were not resting in peace, but were being tormented by demons.

So death was feared more than ever. Men and women, no matter how old, how feeble, how ill, clung desperately to the last flicker of life. And the young doctor, Asclepius, found himself working all day and most of the night. The very old, who were now refusing to die, prevented him from spending enough time among the young. This development, he felt, struck at the very core of his work; for more than any other physician, he had been able to save the lives of men and women in their prime, youths, and a multitude of children.

Using an enormous range of skills to salvage those felled by war or accident, he had snatched them from the very brink of death and restored them to health and beauty and the enjoyment of life.

But there were only so many hours to the day and to the night, and time spent by the bedside of a terrified oldster meant that some young patient, lacking medical attention, would slip into death and be handed over to the demons.

Asclepius . . . was young and strong; he trained himself to sleep less and less.

Asclepius, though, was young and strong; he trained himself to sleep less and less. So he was able to treat all who needed him, and save so many lives that Hades took note. He summoned Hecate.

"Our shipments are dwindling daily," he said. "Do you know why?"

"Fewer people are dying, my lord."

"That much I am able to deduce for myself. The question is, Why aren't they dying as adequately as before? Do you have any ideas, or are you waiting for me to have one?"

"As you know, my Master, the Orpheus affair has taken me to earth frequently. And word has reached me of a certain doctor up there who is performing miraculous cures."

"Who is this quack?"

"His name is Asclepius . . . a son of Apollo, they say."

"Is he?"

"Who knows," said Hecate. "These days, every village wife who bears a good-looking child is rumored to have entertained a god. And, since the rumor is flattering, she doesn't deny it."

"Well, it makes a difference," said Hades. "If he is Apollo's son he'll be harder to get rid of. I'll do what I have to do, but I'd rather not start any family feuds."

"I was about to suggest, your Majesty, that my Harpies may be useful in this matter. If we set a night and day guard upon Asclepius and assign a Harpy to accompany him on each house call, why then she can hover invisibly over the bedside, and as the doctor tries to fan the spark of life, our Harpy, still invisible, can reach out and snuff it. Asclepius will just think he has lost the contest, as sometimes he must, and proceed to the next patient, where the same thing will happen. And again, and again, until even he grows discouraged."

"Sounds good," said Hades. "Send out your hags."

Now, of late, Asclepius had been aided in his labors by a wonderfully beautiful and gentle girl, named Telesphora. She adored the doctor but knew she wouldn't be able to do anything about it until he was less busy. Whereupon, she was able to turn her love into healing energy, and to develop a unique skill. She learned to drain herself of strength each day and lend that strength to patients to carry them through the night—always the most dangerous time for those very ill. And, each morning, her strength renewed itself, and she was ready for that day's task.

She accompanied Asclepius everywhere. Her strong hands became magically gentle when they touched a sufferer's body; a vital force flowed through her fingers and into the sick body. And, despite the Harpies, who were now hanging over each bedside, trying to push the dying one over the brink, despite these invisible hags, Asclepius and his beautiful nurse were saving more lives than ever.

Hades grew so angry that he threatened to demote Hecate and put a vicious crone, Podarge, in charge of the Harpies.

"Give me one more chance, O master," pleaded Hecate. "I'll go up there myself, and if I can't do something to mend matters, why, you won't have to demote me. I'll simply vanish from your sight forever."

The whip coiled at Hecate's belt had a lash that was the tail of a stingray. Wielded by the Harpy Queen, it could scourge the flesh from the bones of anyone she flogged. But she rarely used it. Her claws and teeth were weapons enough; her long sleek body had the fluid brutality of a saber-toothed tiger. Rarely did she meet any difficulty in killing or capturing or punishing anyone she wished.

It puzzled her mightily now that she seemed unable to kill Telesphora.

For she was trying to kill the girl who was so skillfully aiding Asclepius. Even with the young woman's help, the great doctor was working himself to exhaustion, and Hecate knew that if she could deprive him of Telesphora, he would not be able to save so many people.

When the Harpy Queen had told Hades what she meant to do, he issued certain instructions. "Yes, kill her," he said. "But it must seem like an accident. You mustn't attack her in your own form because everyone knows you work for me. And Asclepius will complain to his father, Apollo, who will complain to Zeus, causing endless trouble."

"I'll be careful," Hecate had promised. "She'll soon meet with a fatal but natural-looking accident."

But this proved easier to promise than to perform.

Hecate studied her quarry carefully before determining what accident should take place. The girl went out on the river frequently to gather a certain watercress that Asclepius made into a poultice for cuts and bruises. So death by drowning seemed a good idea.

After further observation, however, Hecate changed her mind about drowning the girl. "It won't work," she thought. "She swims like a naiad, damn her. I'll have to try some other way."

The next day, Telesphora climbed a cliff to hunt for a moss that grew in high places. Hecate followed her. She hovered invisibly as the girl wandered near the edge of the cliff. Then she

Telesphora was able to turn her love into healing energy . . . a vital force flowed through her fingers and into the sick body.

dropped out of the sky, hitting Telesphora with all her weight, knocking the girl off the ledge. And was amazed to see her turn while falling and dive cleanly into the water—then bob up and swim toward shore as if she had gone off a low rock instead of a high cliff.

But Hecate was hard to discourage. Being thwarted made her angry; rage sharpened her purpose. "To be crushed by falling rock would seem a natural fatality for a mountain-climbing lass," she said to herself.

She waited until Telesphora was climbing another slope. Then, scooping up a boulder, Hecate sprang into the air, and hung invisibly above the girl. She dipped so low she couldn't miss, and dropped the boulder. As Hecate watched, the rock plunged through the shining air, then amazed her by skidding away from the neatly braided head as if glancing off an invisible helmet. The heavy rock crashed to the ground near Telesphora, who looked up, startled—and, seeing nothing, continued on her way.

Hecate was scorched by rage, and knew that only blood could cool her. She trembled with pent fury, wanting to swoop down on the girl and dig her talons into that glowing body. But she remembered Hades' instructions, and managed to control herself.

"Eurydice was lucky too until her luck ran out," gritted Hecate. "I'll get this smug bitch if it's the last thing I do. . . . I know! I'll send the same snake that stung Eurydice to death. In fact, I'll send two."

She uttered the snake call, a thin hissing sound. A pair of grass-green vipers whipped out of a hole and slithered toward Telesphora, so swiftly that they were upon her before she knew they were there.

Hecate watched, gloatingly. These were earth's most poisonous snakes. Once they sank their hollow teeth into the girl and injected her with their venom, she would stiffen before she could scream, die before hitting the ground.

She looked like a living caduceus—the serpent-entwined staff of healing carried by Asclepius.

Hecate heard the girl laugh. Saw her stretch out her bare arms. The snakes were climbing and twining about her. Her rosy, laughing face was flanked by two wedge-shaped heads that wove about her, tongues flicking, as if whispering into her ear. She looked like a living caduceus—the serpent-entwined staff of healing carried by Asclepius.

The girl, wound about with snakes, was twirling on her toes, singing. Finally, she plucked them off, playfully braiding them about each other, and flung them away. They untwined themselves and whisked back into their holes.

Hecate knew she would have to do something with her rage or find herself defying Hades' direct order—falling upon the girl and ripping her to pieces where she stood.

Hecate flew off the hill and into the forest. She searched until she found a bear, which she immediately attacked. Locked in a deadly embrace, they rolled over and over, wrestling, biting, gouging. When the Harpy rose to her feet the bear was a heap of bloody fur.

She dived into the river and cleansed herself of blood. Letting herself dry in the hot sun, she grew calm enough to resume her task.

"This is ridiculous," she thought. "I'm being less than I can be. What good are my diabolical wits, honed in the very fires of hell, if I act like a stupid human, befuddled by failure, reacting instead of thinking? I've been on the wrong course with this girl. I see now that she cannot be harmed in any ordinary way, because he whom she serves, Asclepius, son of Apollo, has invoked his father's aid and cloaked her with an immunity. Which means that I shall have to attack her as if she were not quite mortal, but one of those superhuman creatures, hero or monster, who can only be defeated by turning its own strength against itself."

"And what good is Telesphora's special strength, her unique attribute? Why does Asclepius value her so? It is because she has the ability to lend a dying person her own energy, keeping the patient alive, and then somehow being able to renew that energy in herself. I can use this! I can destroy her through her own virtue. I know just how to do it."

Whereupon, Hecate scrolled her wings so that they hung about her like a shabby cloak. She stooped, making herself dwindle, making her skin parch. She retracted her claws and pouched her eyes, dulling their yellow fire—and wrapped the stingray lash of her whip about its stock so that it became just a cane used by a crone.

Transformed into a feeble old woman, the Harpy Queen hobbled off to the hospital Asclepius had built upon the riverbank. There she pretended to collapse. She fell on the grass, and waited for someone to come.

Telesphora bent over the old woman who had been found in the garden. The girl had laid her on a pallet in one of the huts made of woven branches. Sequins of light slid across the ceiling,

Transformed into a feeble old woman, the Harpy Queen hobbled off to the hospital Asclepius had built upon the riverbank.

for one side of the hut was a wide door opening onto the sunlit river. The girl studied the old woman—the strange ashen face, the yolky eyes and shriveled shoulders. She seemed neither awake nor asleep, had not spoken, nor even moaned. Asclepius was away and would not return until the next day. The girl did not know whether the old woman would last, nor could she tell what was ailing her. For all her seeming weakness, her pulse was oddly strong. And yet . . . Asclepius had taught the girl that no two people were exactly alike, and that illness was always more than its symptoms.

One thing she did know. She would get no sleep that night. She would have to sit up with the old woman and be prepared to keep her alive by a transfer of energy.

Now, through eyes that seemed shut, Hecate was studying the girl who was studying her. The Harpy screwed her eyes tight so that no gleam of joy might show. For her plan was working, and soon, soon, Telesphora would deliver herself into the hands of her enemy.

Hours later, in that coldest, clammiest grip of night, just before dawn, Telesphora found herself shuddering with a dread she had never felt before. All night long she had sat beside the bed, letting her strength drain into the body of her patient. She was accustomed to this; this was her talent, her unique virtue, but it had never been quite like this before. The old carcass seemed to be soaking up strength like a sponge, claiming every last particle of energy. And the girl needed to save one drop of vitality so that she might renew herself in the morning.

Telesphora heard a rustling—a different kind of breathing. She tried to stand up. Too late! She felt a pair of claws fasten on her throat. Her eyes widened in horror as she saw the hag sitting up in bed. The limp cloak had become wings, spread like a falcon's, and the eyes, the pouched old eyes were pools of yellow fire.

These blazing eyes were the last sight the girl saw; the last sound she heard was a screech of triumph as the Harpy finished strangling her.

9

The Singing Head

Telesphora slipped out of the vaporous file of shades that were being led toward Hades' judgment seat. She watched them vanish into the mist, then struck off in a different direction across a great hushed plain. She groped through the thick mist, which was not quite fog but a brownish murk, smelling of sulphur.

She kicked something that cried out in pain. She bent to see. It was a head standing on a stump of neck. It was not a skull. Parchment skin stuck to whittled bones. The pale face was framed by a fall of thick, shining white hair. Eyes and mouth were holes, but the eyeholes streamed light, and the voice that issued from the mouth hole was pure radiant power—like sunlight made into sound. Telesphora felt herself fill with a rapture she had never expected to feel again.

"Who are you?" she cried, "whose voice is of such wondrous beauty?"

"I am Orpheus," said the head. "Or, rather, what is left of him."

"Orpheus? And do I hear your voice? Truly, hell has its privileges."

"But who are you?" said the head. "*What* are you? Are you sure you're quite dead?"

"Why do you doubt it?"

"You give off a strange glow—like phosphorus on the night tide. You shed a fragrant warmth that ghosts do not."

"They think I'm dead," said Telesphora. "They tried their best to make me so. But it's your story I want to hear, minstrel. How did you get to be the way you are? Where's the rest of you?"

"I am Orpheus," said the head.
"Or, rather, what is left of him."

"Well, I'll tell you my tale, and you'll tell me yours."

"Oh, yes! Yes!" cried Telesphora.

"One moonlit night," said the head, "I was singing to a party of young women, revelers, you know, who followed Dionysius as he trod the Thracian slopes, fattening the vines. I was singing to them, and they were dancing, when Artemis, acting for the Council of the Gods, poisoned her moon rays, sending the women mad. They fell on me and tore me to pieces. They didn't realize how they were being used, poor creatures; they thought they were applauding my performance. And one of them, a very young one, ran off with my head; she intended to keep it among her dolls. But she was struck by lightning, and my head was taken to this place—and here I've been ever since."

"But why?" whispered Telesphora. "Why were the gods so cruel to you?"

"I had offended them," said the head. "My gifts were my undoing. I was born to sing, and I sang tales of the gods and goddesses, their deeds, their passions, their pets, their victims. My songs pleased men and women and children—oh, they pleased the children—but the gods were not pleased."

"Why not? Why not?"

"My praise was not absolute, you see. I told their cruelty as I celebrated their power. I sang triumphs and crimes. For truth to me is always in motion, aquiver with opposing elements, like everything alive. And the truth I sang was a celebration of total nature, which contains both good and evil. I believed that this huge, rich pageant, human and divine, was a metaphor for something above and beyond, or, perhaps, below and beyond our comprehension—all-embracing, mysteriously inclusive, sublimely total. Unknowable, perhaps, but *not* immune to questions. Thus my song. Thus I offended the gods who like their hosannas loud and simple."

"Why then have they preserved your head, which, it would seem, must continue to offend?"

"Those wildly wasteful gods can be thrifty when it suits them. Disliking me though they did, they found a terrible use for my talent. It started while I was yet alive. And it had to do with their idea of justice—which is a prolongation of punishment."

His voice faded.

"Tell! Tell!" cried Telesphora.

"I haven't spoken so much in decades. I grow weak."

Swiftly, Telesphora stuck her finger in her mouth and bit it sharply. It did not bleed. She grasped the finger with her other hand and squeezed. A drop of blood appeared. The head tilted back. She held her hand so that the blood dripped into the mouth hole.

"Thank you," whispered the voice. "Now I know I'm right about you. Ghosts have no blood."

The girl bit her finger again and squeezed out more blood. The head sipped again, then said "Thank you" in a voice grown strong, and so beautiful, so resonant with tales untold, that Telesphora understood why fish had risen from the depths to listen, why animals had come out of the forest, and trees had hobbled after him on twisted roots.

"Tell on, I pray," whispered Telesphora.

"Where was I?"

"You were saying how the gods found a terrible use for your talents while you were yet alive."

"Oh, yes," spoke the head. "You see, ghosts can die too. They die when they are forgotten. At the precise moment that they vanish from memory, they vanish also from Tartarus. Now, this is intolerable for the gods who have prescribed eternal torment for the dead. Therefore did Hades decree that a minstrel was to be provided. He was to be taken alive, brought down here to witness the ordeal of the damned, and then sent back to the upper world to sing of what he had seen—thus, keeping memory green, and keeping the tortured ghosts conscious of pain."

"And you were the minstrel they chose?"

"I was. They killed my wife, Eurydice, and tempted me down here while I was yet alive, implanting me with the hope that I might bring her out of this place. I came down and saw what was to be seen, and was tricked out of my wife and returned to the upper world to bear witness—precisely as they wished me to. So that now, preserved in my song, Sisyphus still rolls his stone, and starving Tantalus snaps at fruit that sways away from his mouth."

"And that is why they want your head here now—to keep bearing witness?"

"That is why," said Orpheus. "My voice has outlived my body, and this head is its vault—which Hecate has preserved

"They killed my wife, Eurydice, and tempted me down here . . . implanting me with the hope that I might bring her out of this place."

against decay so that it can roll about among the racks, the wheels, the dungeons, and the fire pits. My testimony, drifting up from these chasms, enters the wind and whispers among the treetops, making the river reeds shudder with its tale. Fishermen hear it, men drinking, girls bathing. They tell it to others. It grows with repetition, so that every generation is taught anew of man's duty and the gods' vengeance. But you weep, you weep, beautiful, warm, fragrant, undead girl—you weep!"

His voice was fading again. Because she had no more blood to give him, she scooped up the head and held it to hers. Orpheus drank her tears, and his voice grew strong again. She stood there in the vast murky plain, cradling the head. Holding him like that, she told him about her life on earth. About the great doctor, Asclepius, and the way he saved people from death, and how she had helped him. She told Orpheus how she had taught herself to drain her strong body of its strength and let the vital energy soak into the dying so that they might revive—and how she would renew herself in the morning. Finally she told him how she had been surprised by an old woman who had pretended to be ill, had claimed her last bit of energy—and then, when she was too weak to defend herself, had strangled her.

"It's as I thought," said Orpheus. "You're not quite dead. You must have a god or goddess in your lineage somewhere, and have inherited a freakish spark of immortality. That is why that false hag—who sounds much like Hecate, incidentally—could not quite kill you."

"Well, alive or dead, I'm here," said Telesphora. "And must make the most of it."

"No, my girl," said Orpheus. "What you must do is try to escape. The torments here are bad enough for those dulled by death; for the living they would be unbearable."

"I am here," said Telesphora. "And where there is so much suffering I shall find occupation. But this place is so vast, so dark . . . I'll find my way about, though."

"You must have struck off on your own right after crossing the Styx," said Orpheus. "You cannot have visited Lethe's fountain, or you wouldn't be remembering your life on earth."

"What is this fountain?"

"A gushing spring tended by a nymph named Lethe. The newly dead are taken there first and are served a cupful of oblivion."

"I don't understand."

"In Lethe's fountain run the waters of forgetfulness. One drink and the shade forgets his life on earth, forgets those he loved and who loved him—and is able to enter upon his new ordeal without rancor or regret. It is the only kindness he will know in this place."

"I'll go there now," said Telesphora.

"To drink the waters?"

"No, I shan't drink. I want to remember, not forget. But I also want to see everything that happens down here."

"You are absolutely resolved upon this?"

"I am."

"Then I shall be your guide," said the head. "I know every corner of this damned realm. I'll roll before you as you go."

"Won't you be punished for helping me?"

For the first time, Orpheus smiled. "What can they do to me that has not yet been done?" he asked.

The head pivoted on its neck and rolled away. Telesphora followed.

10

The Rebel Shade

elesphora, somehow, provided herself with a huge water skin, the kind that caravaning merchants used when making a long journey across a dry place. She took the water skin to Lethe's fountain and began to fill it. Lethe saw what the strange shade was doing; she was about to protest, but forgot the matter before she could say anything. For she drank from her own fountain, and was very forgetful.

Then, Telesphora found the ghost of a horse so faithful that when its master was killed in battle it had leaped off a cliff, ending its own life so that it might follow him to Tartarus. But the warrior ghosts had forgotten their feuds and fought no battles, and the war-horse had little now to do and was glad to be pressed into service by Telesphora.

She draped the water skin over the horse's withers and, guided by the head of Orpheus, set off to visit the tormented. Orpheus understood the dreadful risk she was running, but also knew that he would not be able to dissuade her. So he led her to where the torments were worst.

She visited Tantalus, who had been denied food and drink until he was wild with hunger and parched with thirst. He stood in a stream of crystal water under apple trees whose boughs,

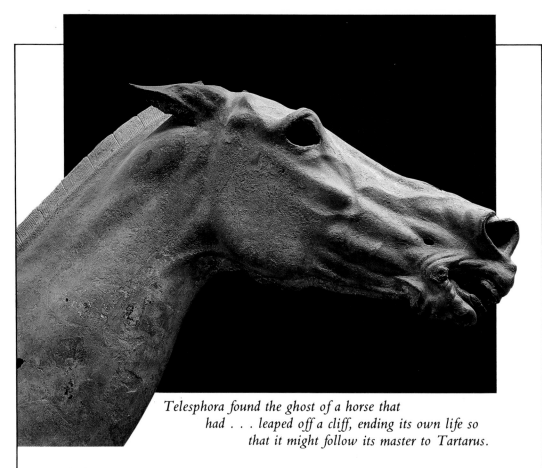

Telesphora found the ghost of a horse that had . . . leaped off a cliff, ending its own life so that it might follow its master to Tartarus.

laden with delicious fruit, bent invitingly toward him. But when he tried to reach for an apple, the boughs swayed gently away, keeping their fruit just out of reach, and he could never eat. But worst of all was thirst. When he bent to the crystal pool, the waters shrank away from his lips, and he could not drink a drop. There he stood, waist-deep in sparkling water under the apple trees, eternally reaching for the fruit, eternally stooping to drink, and eternally denied. Was denied again, but forgot again, and hoped again.

Telesphora wet her hand with Lethe's water and flicked her fingers at Tantalus. A drop fell on his parched lips, and he immediately forgot all the times he had been refused food and drink. Now, when he reached for an apple or stooped for the water, he did so with fresh hope.

"Take me somewhere else!" cried Telesphora.

"Have you really helped him?" asked Orpheus.

"He'll still suffer," said the girl, "but perhaps a little less. And where suffering is concerned, my doctor teaches, a little less is more than it seems."

The head rolled on and led Telesphora to a hill, which was the site of a unique punishment. Here, a man named Sisyphus, hated by the gods, had been condemned to roll a huge stone up the hill. But each time, just as the summit was reached, the rock rolled back, and he had to resume his task at the bottom of the slope and so on through eternity.

When Telesphora approached, she saw him just as he was reaching the summit. His back was bowed, his mighty arms braced, his legs pushing. The rock stopped. The man's legs were working so hard his feet dug into the slope. The rock began to roll backward. The man could not stop it. It gathered speed. It would have rolled over him had he not flung himself hurriedly out of the way.

Telesphora came closer. She saw the man walking slowly downhill after the rock that had now reached the bottom—saw hopeless pain on his face. She dipped out a cupful of Lethe's water. Sisyphus looked at her blankly. Gently, she made him drink it. His face lighted up. Eagerly, he approached the rock and began to push it uphill, as if for the first time.

Orpheus and the girl and the horse watched as Sisyphus rolled the rock up again. They watched the rock slow down, come to a halt. The man struggled with the rock. They watched him follow the rock as it rolled down. But now he wore no look of agony. He looked determined and slightly eager, like one about to attempt a task for the first time.

She visited Tantalus, who had been denied food and drink until he was wild with hunger and parched with thirst.

Telesphora was punished in the cruelest
way possible—through her compassion.
She became witness to ceaseless
agony, and could not look away.

"You see, this is what the doctor told me," said the girl to the head as they left the hill. "The essence of torment is hopelessness—endless performance of the same action without result. But forgetting restores hope and eases pain. Whom do we visit next?"

Orpheus didn't have time to answer. He heard the sound he had been fearing most: brass wings clattering, brass claws chiming, and the savage shriek of Harpies hunting. The horse reared up and galloped away.

Two hags dived upon Telesphora. They lifted her into the air and flew away with her.

She was taken to the Judgement Seat. Hades sat on his ebony throne, listening silently as Hecate charged the girl with the most serious crime that can be committed in hell: Dispensing Forbidden mercies. And the assembled demons howled with glee as Hades declared her guilty and pronounced sentence.

The Harpies, led by Hecate, immediately took her to the deepest part of Tartarus and chained her to a shaft of rock. She was shackled in such a way that she could not move her head. Nor could she close her eyes, for they were propped open with splinters.

And so, Telesphora was punished in the cruelest way possible—through her compassion. She was forced to watch someone being tormented in an unspeakable manner. She became witness to ceaseless agony, and could not look away.

11

The Descent

lthough he had known her only a short time, Orpheus had learned to love the vibrant spirit that was Telesphora. And he could not bear what was happening to her.

"If Asclepius is really a son of Apollo," he thought, "perhaps he can get his father to help."

So Orpheus tried to send a message to the doctor in the only way he knew—through song. His voice entered the waters of the Phlegethon, was carried by underground streams into the river that flowed through the hospital grounds of Asclepius, and invaded the doctor's dreams.

A head floated into his sleep, and he heard a voice of such power and beauty that he felt his bones melting.

"Telesphora needs you!" called the voice. "A spark of life still burns in your murdered girl. But pain will quench it unless you can pluck her out of the bowels of hell."

Not knowing whether he was awake or asleep, but knowing that it didn't matter, Asclepius arose from his pallet and went out into the summer night. The head had vanished, but he could still hear the voice singing, and he followed the lingering sound. Through forest and field he followed the voice as it wound its way among birdcall. Nor did he lose it in the pounding of the surf as it led him along the shore, nor in the howling of the wind as he struck inland and began to climb a mountain.

Up one mountain, down another, through a valley, up the next mountain to the dry bed of a lake, and across that stony lake bed to the mouth of a yawning chasm, which he didn't know was Avernus. But he realized it must be the secret entrance to Hades' realm, known only to Orpheus.

The doctor hadn't eaten or slept since leaving his bed in Thessaly. The thought of Telesphora filled him with a bitter energy, and he did not allow himself to grow weary. Into the chasm he descended. The deeper he went the darker it grew, until he was groping in total darkness. He heard a thin twittering. Heard leathery wings flapping close to his head. Felt claws skimming his hair. He picked up two stones and clapped them together as he walked. For the keen-eared bats, he knew, disliked loud noises.

All this time, he was following the thread of Orpheus' song, winding up to him from far below.

He heard a thin twittering. Heard
leathery wings flapping close to his head.

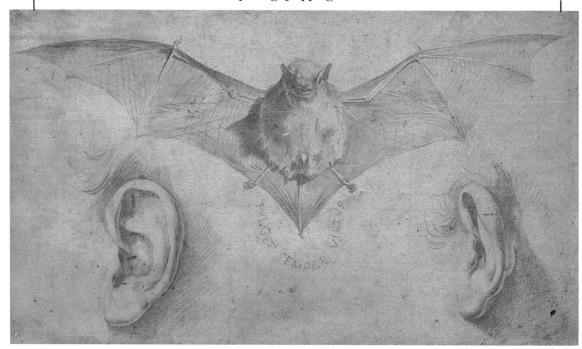

Finally, the path seemed to level off; blackness grew brown. A brown fog swirled about him. He came out of the cave and was in the open now. A wind blew, laden with mist, tinged with the smell of sulphur. It blew the fog into tatters, but Asclepius still had difficulty seeing where he was going. Something gleamed near his feet. He stooped and saw that it was a pair of eyes, and that the eyes were in a head that stood on a stalk of neck, the same head that had floated into his dreams.

And the same melodious voice said, "Welcome, doctor."

"Greetings, Orpheus. Thank you for leading me here. But how cold this mist is. It chills me to my marrow. I thought hell was hot."

"A common delusion. Hell is cold—not specifically, but indifferently. Only our roasting pits are hot."

"Do I see lights far off?" asked Asclepius.

"That is the pearl and crystal roof of our lord's palace, in Erebus. In the great throne room sit Hades and Persephone. Huge, black-robed, and terrible is Hades, receiving the twittering petitions of the drifting dead—which he always ignores."

"Is that where we're going?"

"It's a splendid sight, but I do not recommend it. You are an intruder here. If discovered, you will be horribly punished. There is a pleasant sound of bells in the dusk of those palace grounds, but that chiming is made by the brass wings of Harpies, whose queen is Hecate. Should they sniff a living mortal—and with all due respect, your spoor is strong, brother, carnally strong—if they should sniff you out, they would swoop upon you, seize you in their brass claws, and scourge the flesh from your bones with their stingray whips. However, I know a way to bypass the palace."

"Never has detour seemed more attractive."

"This way then," said the head.

They went in silence until they came to a broad cypress-lined avenue. "This is the Road Away," said the head. "We must follow it."

Asclepius saw shapes beneath the trees. They stood in a silent double row, facing each other.

"What are they?" he whispered. "Sentries?"

"Statues. Come, we must pass between them."

The head rolled swiftly, leading Asclepius through the aisle of statues. He followed very slowly. A strange reluctance clogged his pace. He felt the air grow thick and resistant, as if he were pushing through an invisible hedge. A torpor invaded him. He looked up into the stone faces. They were in pairs — middle-aged men and women, mostly, who stood upon their pediments, facing each other. Some were younger, some older, but most were in their middle years. He saw that the couples were looking at each other out of their stony eye pits. They were carved of dark marble, stiff and lifeless, but it was their stares, he knew, meeting in midair, that made the space between them so resistant.

"We must take another way," he cried. "I cannot pass between."

"You must. It is the only way."

"Who are they? Why do they glare at each other so?"

"They are those who, in life, turned each other to stone."

"I don't understand," said Asclepius.

"You have heard the story, no doubt, of the young sculptor favored by Aphrodite because he carved one hundred statues of beautiful young girls and gave every one of them her face and form. Finally, he fell in love with the most beautiful statue of all—and was going mad trying to make it respond. But Aphrodite was so pleased to know that even a marble likeness of herself could rob a man of his wits, that she turned the statue into a living girl, and made the sculptor happier than any mortal had ever been. His name was Pygmalion, and hers, Galatea."

"A charming tale," said Asclepius. "But what does it have to do with these statues here?"

"These people were Pygmalions in reverse. They chose each other as mates, lived with each other—but in time, froze each other's responses. They took warm living creatures and turned

"Aphrodite turned the statue into a living girl,
and made the sculptor happier than any mortal
had ever been. His name was Pygmalian."

them into stone. Now, having shed their mortal casing, they are imprisoned in marble effigies of their own deed, and must stand face to face through eternity, staring at each other in silent reproach."

Asclepius was weeping. Hot tears burned his face. But the sadness of the tale turned his attention from himself. His torpor fled. He was filled again with bitter salt energy, and walked swiftly, following Orpheus between the statues.

A cold wind blew. The cypress needles clashed. There was another sound—low and hollow. Asclepius stopped, aghast. "They speak!" he cried. "The statues speak!"

"It is the wind whistling through their earholes," said Orpheus.

"It sounds like voices saying, 'No! No!' "

"That is the word they spoke most often while alive," said Orpheus. "It is the only word left to them now."

Asclepius stopped again. He was standing between two taller statues of extraordinary beauty—a young man and a young woman, and even in cold hard stone, their faces glowed with quenchless vitality. A light clung to the carved faces as if a rosier marble had been used. Both wore short tunics. The man held a leaf-bladed hunting spear. The woman held the collar of a stone hound, lithe as a panther.

"Come," said Orpheus. "I pray you, hasten. We are still too near the palace grounds."

But Asclepius could not stop looking at the marble woman. Her legs were so long, so suavely powerful. The cant of her shoulder and the thrust of her hip as she held the great dog reminded him of Telesphora, and he began to weep once more. The hot tears fell on the stone feet. He wrenched himself away and stumbled on.

"I hate this place," he said.

"Of course," said the head. "That's the idea."

The avenue wound among cypresses. There were no more statues. The head rolled faster and Asclepius picked up his pace. He heard a rumbling and whirled in his tracks. The statue of the woman was walking after him. Her live feet had broken the stone; her big, bare, sinewy feet were stepping through the dust on the road. Pieces of marble still clung to them—like eggshell to a new chick. The stone dog ran alongside. Behind them strode the statue of the man.

Asclepius could not stop looking at the marble woman. Her legs were so long, so suavely powerful.

Asclepius paused. They approached and stopped. He was flanked by two towering stone figures. They looked down at him.

"Thank you, stranger," said the young woman in her windharp voice. "The hot juice of your compassionate heart overflowed your eyes and awakened my feet from their stone sleep. I have come off my pedestal to abide with you as you walk your dire ways."

"I abandoned her in life," boomed the stone man. "Where she goes now, there must I also go, through every avenue of hell. I thank you also, live little fool, who comes at your own invitation. And shall abide with you in dire ways."

"Come!" called the head. They moved on.

12

A Hellish Battle

Walking between the statues of hunter and huntress, Asclepius followed the head as it threaded its way among shafts of stone. The huge pillars of rock thrust straight up and lost themselves in darkness. Asclepius didn't know it, but he was moving among those spurs of rock belonging to the root system of Olympus.

Chained upright to the most massive of these pillars was a naked body towering higher than the tallest tree. Its ceaseless sobbing was like wind in the top branches of a cedar. Harpies wheeled about the great bearded face. They had long since torn out his eyes, but dipped, sipping at the blood, which welled like tears out of the empty sockets.

"Who?" whispered Asclepius.

"Tityus," said the head of Orpheus. "Mightiest of the ancient Titans, who led a revolt against Zeus."

Asclepius breathed a foul stench. The Harpies had torn the Titan's stomach open and were gorging themselves on the stinking viscera—which grew again, as they were being eaten, so that his pain might never cease.

"Come," said the head. "We must pass under him."

"Why?"

"She whom you seek is in the deepest part of Hades' realm, called Tartarus. And the Titan's legs frame the portal of that place."

The head rolled on. And as Asclepius followed, he knew that he was entering the entrails of hell.

The air darkened. The heavy sulphurous light became tan, then brown; there was a smell of smoke, but no flicker of flame. Asclepius toiled on. The head rolled before him. The stone couple and the stone dog rumbled behind.

He heard men and women screaming, demons laughing. Agonized rattling screams that became small, helpless, puppy-like whimperings. The laughter was wild and mirthless, rising as the screams died. Asclepius froze. He could go no farther. The head rolled back.

"This is no place to stop and gawk, my friend! Spectators are too often persuaded to play more active roles."

"Is this the place of torment?" asked Asclepius.

"One of them," answered the head.

"Who is screaming so dreadfully?"

"The younger brother of Tityus, who also conspired against Zeus. We are coming to his site of punishment."

"I don't want to see it."

"Unfortunately, she whom you seek is also there."

The head rolled swiftly on. Asclepius raced to follow, and came upon the worst sight he had ever seen. Chained to a shaft of rock was a magnificent young Titan being eaten by a serpent. Although his capacity for pain was as limitless as his strength had been, his pride was even stronger, and he was trying to bite back his screams as the huge speckled serpent twined about him, devouring his flesh. Through his horror and outrage, Asclepius felt his doctorly instincts stirring, and found himself studying the anatomy of the Titan's ordeal.

Being of divine stock, the Titan could not wholly die, but his flesh was not wholly renewed, and Asclepius recognized that the spectacle of his own mutilation would be a special cruelty to the beautiful young giant who had exulted so in the strength of his body. Thus it was that he had lost an arm and a leg. His head was intact, but the thorax had been eaten away; only the mighty spool of his backbone linked the mangled cavity of his chest to his pelvis.

The serpent twined, weaving colors; grey melted into green, and tan into grey again—a looping, sliding dance of colors, climaxed by a smooth thrust of tapered head as it touched the Titan and pulled away, swallowing a gobbet of flesh. And then, Asclepius saw something even more horrifying.

Beyond Titan and serpent was Telesphora, shackled to another pillar of rock. Asclepius heard her moaning. He drew his sword.

"Put it back!" said Orpheus. "That beast will take you in one gulp, like a grass snake eating a frog."

"I have to do something!"

"Not with a sword. That is Hades' own serpent, the simplified shape of evil. It moves faster than the eye can see. If you come near, it will cast a single loop, wrap you in a cable of living muscle, drag you to its maw, and swallow you alive. You will not even be granted the boon of fangs, but feel your bones pulping on the way down."

"Nevertheless," said Asclepius, "I must do what I can."

Again he raised his sword.

"No!" cried Orpheus. "Let me try something first. Once, when I was young, courting a nymph who lived in Libya, I was attacked by a tiger. I had no weapon but my lyre. I began my song as the beast crouched to spring—a lullaby, so slumberous the tiger fell asleep. He slept until I awakened him, then followed me like a house cat. I know my voice has become rusty, but let me see what I can do."

Asclepius lowered his sword. The head began to sing:

Who quenched your eye and muffled your sense?
Who has enslaved the ancient king?
It was she, she.
She was created before all creation;
Out of her came the first darkness.
She divided into light and darkness.
From her womb flowed snakes of light;
And she named you Ophion or Moon-snake.
Ophion was your name.

Her belly swelled like a storm cloud;
She bore a son who swore to kill you.
You were angry, serpent, with a terrible anger,
Your mother sang to you—a lulling song, a spell;
The wind was in it and the few created things.
The song was a spell, the first charm,
Full of sleep and magic—like bees buzzing,
Like a spinning wheel. She spun life on the wheel,
And you turned it—spun goats, fish, mice.

She cut the earth with a sharp piece of bone,
Your leg bone. Your legs folded
Into your belly. You had to crawl on your belly.
She filled a bladder with moon-fire and mice;
It burst into rain. For forty days,
The moon-fire rained jewels and flowers and tigers.
The mice became demons to serve your angry son.

And that infant, guarded by spiked demons,
Grew apace, maturing in eight days.
On the ninth day he put his heel to your head
And pronounced himself king.
Who quenched your eyes and muffled your sense
And stole your name? Do you know? Do you know?

So Orpheus sang, and the snake seemed to listen. Its loops slackened; it ceased to forage the Titan's raw bones. Its lifted head was weaving slightly to the music.

The statue had moved closer and stood silently, listening.

Who quenched your eyes and stole your name?
Do you know? Do you know?

And, as the beast seemed to be yielding to the honeyed slumber in that magic voice, the head of Orpheus advanced, not rolling in its usual way, because that would have blotted the sound, but hopping on its neck stump.

Ancient sire, fallen king, do you know?
Do you know?

The tapered head swayed heavily, sleepily. Orpheus moved closer, singing. Then slowness melted horribly into speed. The snake's head dipped as the living cable of the 60-foot body uncoiled in a blur of movement. In a loathsome mime of kissing, the rubbery lips moved over the song-rapt bearded face. Asclepius tried to close his eyes, but it happened too fast. He saw the snake swallow the head of Orpheus like a child eating an apple.

Orpheus sang, and the snake seemed to listen. Its lifted head was weaving slightly to the music.

He heard himself yelling. He rushed forward and slashed at the serpent with his sword.

But the blade never touched the mottled scales. The serpent moved too swiftly, sliding away from his blow and casting a single loop about Asclepius, binding his arms to his sides. He felt a paralyzing constriction. The sword fell from his hand. The breath rushed out of his lungs in a moaning gasp, and he could not draw another. The pressure was unbearable. He felt his arms mashing into his ribs. Darkness swarmed.

He heard a rustling, a grinding, a phlegmy scream, and thought, "I am dead. My shade has been taken to the Lake of Fire. I hear the voices of those swimming in the flame."

The pressure eased. Air rushed into his lungs. The loop had slackened. He fell out of the coil. He tried to stand but could not. He coughed and spat blood. He moved his arms. The pain blinded him, but pain pierced his fog. His sight cleared. He pulled his sword to him and, using it as a cane, climbed to his feet. Retching and spitting blood, he leaned against a rock and watched the statues fighting the serpent.

The stone hands of the hunter were clamped about the serpent below its head, and he was trying to throttle the beast. The snake had cast its loops about the statue and was squeezing him to a pulp. Marble had begun to crack off the petrified shade of the dead hero, and Asclepius saw the pink pulsing mist of his spirit at the core of stone.

The huntress was helping her husband. Her tall legs were flexing in a beautiful curve of marble thew as she leaped high

The snake had cast its loops about the statue and was squeezing him to a pulp.

in the air and fell with all her tremendous weight on the middle part of the serpent's body. The stone girl was leaping twice her height and falling upon the giant snake, crushing the thick cable of bone and muscle like a gardener crushing a worm with a spade. Again and again she leaped and dropped, breaking her own body with every fall—until she lay motionless upon the mottled green coils, her stone carapace shattered. The pink mist of her spirit was fuming out and mixing with the hissing blood of the serpent.

All this while the great jaws of the stone dog were savaging the snake, striking here and there, driving stone teeth into leather body.

And the stone man still grappled the monster; it was now a death grip. Blood spurted from the lidless eyes. The tapered head lolled. The coils went slack. The stone man collapsed, tried to rise, but could not. Asclepius watched him drag himself toward the huntress. She pulled herself to her shattered knees and crept toward him.

They stretched out their hands. Both collapsed. With their last strength they reached toward each other. Their hands met, clasped, and were still. These two, hunter and huntress, whose marriage had failed, and whose shades had been frozen into stony shapes of reproach and remorse, staring at each other out of great scooped eyes—these two, wakened from rancorous stupor by the hot tears of a living man, had attached themselves to his deed, and, sanctified by generous risk, had, in their last gesture, annulled their failure. Shells shattered, they forgave each other before an expert witness, departed hell, and entered legend.

Asclepius had no time to mourn them. He ran toward Telesphora, leaping over the fallen statues, trying not to look down at them but unable to avoid a glimpse. He saw that the shattered stone, spirit departed, had lost luster and individuality, and had merged with the rubble of that penitential field.

Asclepius stepped over the coils of the dead serpent and reached Telesphora, who stared at him in wonder. He lifted his sword and struck twice. His blade sheared through her chains.

Tenderly, he drew her out of her shackles. They embraced. "Come . . . let us return to earth," he said.

"Can we really leave?" she whispered. "They'll be after us, won't they, those horrible winged hags?"

"They can't be worse than that serpent. And we escaped him."

"Yes, we did!" cried Telesphora. "Let's go, dear doctor. Let's start."

Hand in hand, they began their journey out of the underworld. Harpies observed them, and reported to Hecate, who hurried to confer with Hades. He listened to her silently, then said:

"What do you propose?"

"To take them, of course," said Hecate.

"Consider this, O Hag. If we keep them down here with their obsessive yen for easing pain and their combined skills, they will always be trying to disrupt our torments. They'll be a constant source of trouble."

"But," said Hecate. "If we allow them to return to earth they will continue to postpone death for their patients, and reduce our intake."

"Only so long as they live," said Hades. "And by the nature of things, that can't be much longer than the mortal span. So if we wait for a bit, they will fall into our hands in a natural way; no fuss, no family quarrels. Yes, we can afford to let them go.

We'll get them back one day. When we do, we'll teach them to regret their damned good works, won't we?"

"We will, master, we will! And perhaps relish our vengeance all the more for the delay."

So Asclepius and Telesphora were allowed to return to earth and take up their practice where they had left off. And, it is told, the doctor began by restoring the girl to full health. It is also told that they interrupted their labors long enough to get married. They had many children and grandchildren, and all of them, legend says, practiced medicine.

What happened later to their shades, we do not know. And, perhaps, we don't want to.

Things have shrunk since then. Giants are freaks; dragons are flies; heroes are sandwiches; monsters eat cookies. Demons have shrunk too, become so tiny that they are invisible, but still plague humankind, more expertly than ever, attacking from within. We don't know where Hecate is, exactly, but Harpies still fly.

And sometimes, when the wind is right, and if we listen very, very, carefully, we can hear the voice of Orpheus singing of things that happened long ago.

Acknowledgments

Letter Cap Illustrations by Hrana L. Janto

Opposite page 1, TWILIGHT OF THE FLYING LIZARD *(1985/86) by Emilio Cruz, oil on canvas (6 x 7')*
  Courtesy of The Artist and Anita Shapolsky Gallery, New York

Page 3, MEPHISTOPHELES *(1947) by Ivan Albright, oil on canvas (80 3/4 x 42")*
  Courtesy of the Sid Deutsch Gallery, New York

Page 5, BLACK, WHITE AND GRAY *by Franz Kline (1910–1962), oil on canvas (105 x 78")*
  Courtesy of The Metropolitan Museum of Art, New York; George A. Hearn Fund, 1959 (59.165)

Page 6, DEMON PULLING ST ANTHONY'S HAIR, *detail from the Isenheim Altarpiece by Matthias Grünewald (ca. 1470–1528)*
  Courtesy of The Musée Unterlinden, Colmar
    Photo: Giraudon/Art Resource, New York

Page 8, PAGAN SACRIFICE *by Toussaint Dubreuil (1560–1602), oil on canvas*
  Courtesy of The Louvre, Paris
    Photo: Scala/Art Resource, New York

Page 10, THE SACRIFICE OF IPHIGENIA *by Carle van Loo (1705–1765), pen and ink and wash over traces of black chalk, on brown-washed paper (28 x 35 7/16")*
  Courtesy of The Metropolitan Museum of Art, New York; Rogers Fund, 1953 (53.121)

Page 11, ORPHEUS CHARMING THE NYMPHS AND ANIMALS *by Charles Natoire (1700–1777), pen and ink with wash and some watercolor on paper*
  Courtesy of The Metropolitan Museum of Art, New York; Robert Lehman Collection, 1975 (1975.1.676)

Page 12, ORPHEUS *by Raoul Dufy (1877–1953), woodcut illustration (no. 18) from Guillaume Apollinaire's* Le Bestiare, *published by Deplanche, Paris, 1911 (ed. of 120/copy 99)*
  Courtesy of The Metropolitan Museum of Art, New York; Harris Brisbane Dick Fund, 1926 (26.92.30)

Page 14, WOMAN IN GREEN *by Pablo Picasso (1881–1974), oil on canvas*
  Courtesy of a private collection, New York
    Photo: Art Resource, New York

Page 17, GRAPE HARVEST WITH PUTTI, *Roman mosaic (ca. 4th century A.D.)*
  Courtesy of Santa Costanza, Rome
    Photo: Scala/Art Resource, New York

Page 18, YOUNG BACCHUS *by Guido Reni (1575–1642), oil on canvas*
  Courtesy of the Galleria Palatina, Florence
    Photo: Scala/Art Resource, New York

Page 20, YOUTH SINGING AND PLAYING THE KITHARA, *red-figured Greek amphora by the Berlin Painter (ca. 490 B.C.), terra cotta (h. 16 3/8")*
  Courtesy of The Metropolitan Museum of Art, New York; Fletcher Fund, 1956 (56.171.38)

Page 23, THE WATHERMAN *by Max Ernst (1891–1976), oil on canvas*
  Courtesy of Ca'Pesaro, Venice
    Photo: Scala/Art Resource, New York

Page 24, REDEYESCAPE *(1985/86) by Emilio Cruz, oil on canvas (4 1/2 x 5 1/2')*
  Courtesy of The Artist and Anita Shapolsky Gallery, New York

Page 26, WINGED DEMON (HECATE?), *detail from* SCENES OF DIONYSIAC RITES *a wall painting (ca. 50 B.C.), Villa of the Mysteries, Pompeii*
    Photo: Scala/Art Resource, New York

Page 28, ORPHEUS AND EURYDICE *by Nicolas Poussin (1593/94–1665), oil on canvas*
  Courtesy of The Louvre, Paris
    Photo: Scala/Art Resource, New York

Page 30, PARNASSUS *by Nicolas Poussin, oil on canvas*
  Courtesy of The Prado, Madrid
    Photo: Scala/Art Resource, New York

Page 32, ORPHEUS AND EURYDICE *by Timothy Woodman (b. 1952), painted aluminum (81 x 36 x 13")*
  Courtesy of The Metropolitan Museum of Art, New York; Hugo Kastor Fund, 1983 (1983.458)

Page 34, ORPHEUS AND EURYDICE, *majolica plate from Italy (16th century)*
  Courtesy of The Metropolitan Museum of Art, New York; Robert Lehman Collection, 1975 (1975.1.1031)

Page 35, GUERILLA WARFARE *(1971/73) by Brad Davis, synthetic polymer and metal leaf on canvas (100 3/4 x 81"/irregular—unframed)*
  Courtesy of The Whitney Museum of American Art, New York; purchase with funds from Mr. and Mrs. William A. Marstellar (Acq.#73.72)
    Photo: Geoffrey Clements

Page 36, UNTITLED, *bronze head (1984/86) by Mary Frank, edition of four (28 x 34 x 22")*
  Courtesy of The Artist and Zabriskie Gallery, New York

Page 38, WOUNDED AENEAS AND THE DOCTOR, *Roman wall painting (ca. 1st century A.D.)*
　　Courtesy of The National Museum, Naples
　　　　Photo: Scala/Art Resource, New York

Page 40, CHIRON TEACHING ACHILLES TO PLAY THE LYRE, *wall painting from the Basilica of Herculaneum (ca. 50 B.C.)*
　　Courtesy of The National Museum, Naples
　　　　Photo: Scala/Art Resource, New York

Page 42, Detail from THE DARK FIGURE *(1938) by Federico Castellón, oil on canvas (17 x 26")*
　　Courtesy of The Whitney Museum of American Art, New York; Purchase (Acq.#42.3)
　　　　Photo: Geoffrey Clements

Page 44, ASCLEPIUS, *Roman sculpture (ca. 2nd century A.D.)*
　　Courtesy of The Museo Capitolino, Rome
　　　　Photo: Alinari/Art Resource, New York

Page 47, Detail from THE ALDOBRANDINE WEDDING BANQUET, *Early Christian mural (ca. 5th century A.D.)*
　　Courtesy of The Vatican Museums
　　　　Photo: Scala/Art Resource, New York

Page 48, THE SNAKE GODDESS *from the temple of Knossos Palace (ca. 1600 B.C.), terra cotta/faience figurine (h. 13 1/2")*
　　Courtesy of The Heraklion Museum, Crete
　　　　Photo: Scala/Art Resource, New York

Page 50, THE JOURNEY *(1940) by Elliot Orr, oil on canvas (10 1/2 x 14 1/2")*
　　Courtesy of The Whitney Museum of American Art, New York; Anonymous Gift (Acq.#53.45)
　　　　Photo: Geoffrey Clements

Page 52, ORPHEUS *by Gustave Moreau (1826–1898), oil on canvas*
　　Courtesy of The Louvre, Paris
　　　　Photo: Lauros-Giraudon, Paris

Page 54, ORPHEUS *by Jean Delville (1867–1953), oil on canvas*
　　Courtesy of The Gillion-Crowet Collection, Brussels
　　　　Photo: Lauros-Giraudon, Paris

Page 57, ORPHEUS AND EURYDICE ON THE BANKS OF THE RIVER STYX *by John Rodham Spencer-Stanhope (1829–1908), oil on canvas*
　　Courtesy of Christie's, New York

Page 60, TEMPERANTIA *by Sir Edward Burne-Jones (1833–1898), oil on canvas*
　　Courtesy of Christie's, London
　　　　Photo: Bridgeman/Art Resource, New York

Page 62, Detail from THE JOCKEY, *Greek bronze (ca. 4th century B.C.)*
　　Courtesy of The National Museum, Athens
　　　　Photo: Nimatallah/Art Resource, New York

Page 63, Detail from THE LAST JUDGMENT: THE DAMNED *by Rogier van der Weyden (1399/1400–1464)*
　　Courtesy of The Hôtel Dieu, Beaune
　　　　Photo: Giraudon/Art Resource, New York

Page 64, Detail from THE INFERNO: UNIVERSAL JUDGMENT *by Fra Angelico (ca. 1400–1455)*
Courtesy of The San Marco Museum, Florence
Photo: Scala/Art Resource, New York

Page 66, MASK OF TRAGEDY, *Roman wall painting (ca. 1st century A.D.)*
Photo: Giraudon/Art Resource, New York

Page 68, STUDIES OF A BAT AND TWO EARS *by Jusepe de Ribera (1591–1652), red chalk and wash on paper (6 1/4 x 11")*
Courtesy of The Metropolitan Museum of Art, New York; Rogers Fund, 1972 (1972.77)
Photo: Bob Hanson

Page 71, PYGMALION AND GALATEA *by Jean-Léon Gérôme (1824–1904), oil on canvas (35 x 27")*
Courtesy of The Metropolitan Museum of Art, New York; Gift of Louis C. Raegner, 1927 (27.200)

Page 71, AMAZON, *Roman copy of a Greek statue (ca. 2nd century A.D), marble*
Courtesy of The Museo Pio Clementino, Vatican
Photo: Scala/Art Resource, New York

Page 74, DEVIL BREAKING A WINDOW, *detail from The Isenheim Altarpiece by Matthias Grünewald*
Courtesy of The Musée Unterlinden, Colmar
Photo: Giraudon/Art Resource, New York

Page 79, COBRA, *one of a pair by Jean du Nand (1877–1942), bronze, partly gilt (h. 12"w. 5 1/2" D. 9')*
Courtesy of The Metropolitan Museum of Art, New York; Rogers Fund, 1970 (1970, 198.7)

Page 80, LAÖCOON GROUP, *Roman copy of Greek original (1st century A.D.) marble (h. 7')*
Courtesy of The Vatican Museums
Photo: Scala/Art Resource, New York

Page 82, THE INSCRIPTION OVER THE GATE OF HELL *by William Blake (1757–1827), illustration from Dante's Divine Comedy, watercolor (20 3/4 x 14 3/4")*
Courtesy of The Tate Gallery, London

BOOKS BY BERNARD EVSLIN

Merchants of Venus
Heroes, Gods and Monsters of the Greek Myths
Greeks Bearing Gifts: The Epics of Achilles and Ulysses
The Dolphin Rider
Gods, Demigods and Demons
The Green Hero
Heraclea
Signs & Wonders: Tales of the Old Testament
Hercules
Jason and the Argonauts